Bowl·O·Rama

THE VISUAL ARTS
OF BOWLING

H. THOMAS STEELE

ABBEVILLE PRESS · PUBLISHERS · NEW YORK

Library of Congress Cataloging in Publication Data

Steele, H. Thomas
Bowl-O-Rama: the visual arts of bowling.

1. Bowling—Collectibles—United States.
2. Bowling—United States—History. I. Title.
GV902.7.S74 1986   794.6′0973   85–30799
ISBN 0–89659–607–9
Editor: Walton Rawls
Design and Principal Photography: H. Thomas Steele

TABLE OF CONTENTS

As for countless other postwar offspring, bowling was a memorable part of my childhood recreation. Although I was never a team or league bowler, many of my family outings and the birthday parties of neighborhood friends included a trip to our local lanes. An average bowler, I threw my share of strikes, spares, and gutterballs, though not necessarily in that order. But something beyond the urge to bowl good scores attracted me to America's most popular participant sport. There was devilish delight in knocking the pins to high heaven, pins that had been so carefully set up in symmetrical alignment. Striking them all down at once was even better. Moreover, this basically destructive act was socially acceptable! I liked the noise factor of bowling as well. The rolling sound of fifteen-pound balls in contact with hardwood floors on their way to imminent collision with plastic-coated wooden pins at speeds approaching 35 miles per hour made echo chambers of bowling alleys. Good body English held until the loud crash added to the primal pleasure. Bowling was also group-oriented, competitive, and an inexpensive exercise. This active/passive sport was the only one where you did not have to chase the ball. It always came back to you. The environment caught my eye, welcomed me, and pulled me in. I have fond memories of Llo-Da-Mar Lanes in Santa Monica with its streamlined modern architecture, its pink and white neon signs and its step-down lanes. It was magical. Sad to say, Llo-Da-Mar has been converted into modern storefronts.

Bowling culture is more alive today than ever, but its visual arts are vanishing. The look, character, and details—the esoteric aesthetics—have changed. The tendency to bulldoze our past, pave it over, and make parking lots, new malls, or highrises is based on economics. Architectural landmarks fall under the wrecking ball as real estate prices escalate. As the outer shell goes, so goes the inner soul. Progress supersedes aesthetics. Bowling may be offbeat, it may be nostalgic, but it also has pride and a great sense of humor. It is pure Americana. Where else in our fast-paced world do we find the weekly camaraderie of the bowling league, with its clever team emblems and humorous logos, a beer in one hand and a ball in the other? What follows is a catalog of popular history and archival fun. This book will strike you right and have you rolling in the gutters. Whether you are an avid kegler or occasionally bowl a few frames, this will be right up your alley. A part of our present always contains a part of our past. So, spare me a few minutes, and let's go bowling!

—H. Thomas Steele

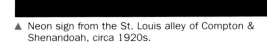

▲ Neon sign from the St. Louis alley of Compton & Shenandoah, circa 1920s.

▶ OPPOSITE: *Profound Object, 1985.* Inspired by Phil Garner; photograph by Dennis Keeley.

Bowling is the harmless sublimation of the terrible human instinct to throw things. No one would have been more skilled at this than early man, who probably threw rocks at small animals to hone his hunting skills for the big game. However, the earliest evidence of man's passion for bowling was unearthed in the 1930s. A British paleontologist, Sir Flinders Petrie, found bowling-related articles in the tomb of an Egyptian child buried near Cairo about 5200 B.C. The primitive playthings found included nine conical stone pins, three stone balls, and three pieces of marble used to make a wicket. There is evidence that the game was also enjoyed by the Greeks around 2000 B.C., and later the Romans, through contacts with Egypt via the Mediterranean. Another discovery was the ancient Polynesian game of *ula maika,* which utilized pins and balls of stone. Amazingly, the distance from ball to pins was approximately 60 feet, the same as today's standard.

Bowling at pins as we know it probably originated in Germany, not as a sport but as a third-century religious rite, according to 19th-century German histo-

▲ Bowling articles discovered by Sir Flinders Petrie in an Egyptian tomb, circa 5200 B.C.

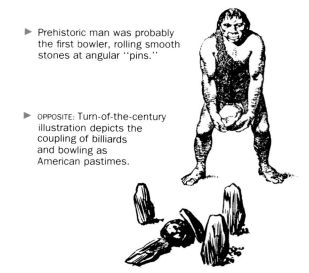

▶ Prehistoric man was probably the first bowler, rolling smooth stones at angular "pins."

▶ OPPOSITE: Turn-of-the-century illustration depicts the coupling of billiards and bowling as American pastimes.

rian William Pehle. Parishioners rolled stones at their *kegel,* a stick carried for sport and self-defense. The kegel, which represented the *heide* or devil, was set up at one end of the church cloisters. Topple the symbolic heide and you were cleansed of sin. In time the stones became larger wooden balls. The German clerical leader Martin Luther was credited with settling on nine as the ideal number of pins in the early 1500s. He even had a bowling lane built for his children. In the Middle Ages bowling had shifted from a religious ritual to a game of competition and fun. It spread into Europe and the lowland countries to the north, where wagering on matches developed. Match entrants would put up chickens, oxen, and venison as prizes instead of money, with winner take all. Sometimes the winner took everything a man had——his food, horses, land, and house. Gambling and rowdiness followed, causing the priests to denounce the game. Controversy over these corollary aspects of the sport led to bans on bowling, though they were seldom observed because of the sport's popularity with nobility and common folk alike.

While most of continental Europe was bowling at pins, the British Isles were taking to *bowles* or lawn bowling, which had evolved from the Italian game of *boccie,* in which you roll a ball at a fixed object. By a royal act of King Henry VIII in 1541, all forms of bowling were outlawed in England for three reasons. The king considered bowling a privilege of the wealthy, who were the only ones able to purchase the newly required license to play. He found that his soldiers were losing their archery skills by skipping practice with the difficult longbow in order to bowl. Thirdly, because of the moral decay of his subjects, he believed that bowling had ceased to be a sport and had become a vicious form of gambling.

Colonists came to the New World with a love of the sport of outdoor bowling in one form or other. In the middle 1600s, Dutch explorers and traders under Henry Hudson were instrumental in introducing a form of pin bowling known as *skittles* or ninepins. British settlers in America played lawn bowls in the area of lower Manhattan still known as Bowling Green. William Penn, writing in 1673, found bowls furnished a "seemly and good diversion." In the 1819 tale by Washington Irving, Rip Van Winkle spied little men playing at ninepins in the mountains and likened thunder to the sound of their balls rolling toward pins.

By the 1830s bowling was flourishing in America. However, many of the problems surrounding the game in Europe soon arose in the New World. The scourge that struck lawn bowling in medieval England—gambling—became the evil of the American bowling scene. Matches held by tavern owners to build up business led to betting and rowdiness and ultimately to laws against the game. A Connecticut legislative act in 1841 circumvented the prohibition

▲ Captured in vintage photographs are men's and women's bowling teams from the early 1900s. Note the black pinboys in the top photograph.

▶ OPPOSITE: Bold typography extolled the popularity of women's bowling in this 1925 poster. The Women's National Bowling Association was formed in 1916, and it later became the Women's International Bowling Congress (WIBC).

Eighth Annual

BOWLING

TOURNAMENT

OF THE

Women's National Bowling Ass'n.

Incorporated

Commencing

APRIL 25, 1925

Entry Fee

$3.00

a Person Each Event

Entries Close

APRIL 4, 1925

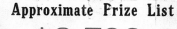

Approximate Prize List

$3,500

Gold Medals

to be awarded for Five-Handed, Two-Handed, Individual and All Event Championships.

$50.00

SPECIAL PRIZE to the Team of Five-Women Traveling the Greatest Number of Miles to Attend This Tournament.

Reduced Rates (Fare and One-Half) On All Railroad Lines

To Be Held at

F. G. Smith Recreation Co. Bowling Alleys

1901-03 East 13th Street, Cleveland, Ohio

For Hotel Reservations, Write Mrs. Grace Garwood, 12905 Superior Ave., Cleveland, Ohio

Mrs. JEAN KNEPPRATH, President
140-23rd Street, Milwaukee, Wis.

Mrs. OLLIE FOSTER, Secretary
5959 Magnolia Avenue, Chicago, Ill.

Mail All Entries With Certified Check, Postoffice Money Order, or Draft Direct to the Secretary

against ninepins by cleverly adding a tenth pin (supposedly for the first time) and arranging the pins into an equilateral triangle. Clever but not a first, since English and Dutch paintings document tenpin alleys well before 1841. Indoor lanes such as Knickerbocker Alleys in Manhattan, which opened in the 1840s, made weather and time factors inconsequential. This alone caused a tremendous rise in the game's growth and popularized the sport.

The expansion of bowling spread westward from Manhattan and the Bronx to Syracuse, Buffalo, Cincinnati, Chicago, Milwaukee, and St. Louis, cities with large German immigrant populations that became bowling strongholds. The Germans contributed good times, camaraderie, and beer to the game. They organized teams and leagues, encouraging even women to bowl. As women took up the sport, out went unsavory spitoons and cursing in public, down went rugs and in came clean-shaven attendants. The derogatory connotations of "alley" caused it to be changed to "lane" and later to "center." The swift emergence of tenpins imbued bowling with newfound

► Bowling became an extremely popular sport in Hawaii for servicemen and natives alike. More than an umbrella was needed during the 1941 bombing of Pearl Harbor—shirt pocket graphics for a credit union bowling team.

► OPPOSITE: 1907 woman's crying towel, with depictions of slang terms for typical bowling situations. Note the scores on the chalkboard; the women are leading.

respectability, since the flagrant gambling image that had tainted ninepins was avoided. The major remaining problem was a lack of uniform playing rules and equipment specifications, stifling development of the game as a whole. As clubs formed and competition (spurred by an eagerness to show off skills) increased, order needed to be instituted out of the resulting chaos. The first attempt at organization led to the National Bowling Association in 1875, which was followed by the short-lived American Bowling League in 1890. Both were futile efforts to standardize the game, although some of the legislation agreed upon became the cornerstone of today's game.

The breach that existed between the New York State bowlers and everyone else to the west was mended by the formation of the American Bowling Congress in 1895. The rules and standards laid down ultimately were adhered to universally, and they have remained basically unchanged ever since. Uniform ball size, more openly spaced pins, and a new scoring system created more of a challenge and gave room for improvement. Bowling became a favorite social activity of many fraternal groups, such as Kiwanis, Elks, Moose, Shriners, B'nai B'rith, and the Knights of Columbus. Since bowling depends more on rhythm and timing than on strength, women joined the sport in record numbers, making more rapid progress than some men. Club challenges sprouted from regional to national events. The 1936 Olympics in Berlin offered

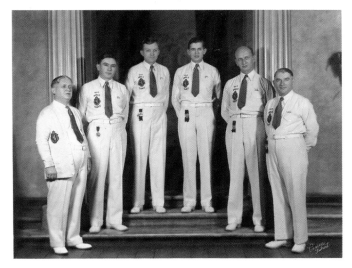

▲ Breweries signed bowling stars to their teams for the comeback of their product after Prohibition. Pictured is the Stroh's Beer Team of Detroit in 1934, famous for their white uniforms.

▲ Commercial businesses sponsored many teams as a form of free advertising and community goodwill. Shown above is the St. Louis Dairy Company's women's team of the 1930s.

bowling competition, and America's Hank Marino won all events.

Bowling proprietors had suffered double trouble in the roaring '20s. Prohibition took away a large source of income for many, and the Great Depression bankrupted the rest. But bowling's resurgence began when Prohibition was repealed in 1933. Breweries needed a mass audience for the comeback of their product, and bowling provided it. "Beer teams" were formed by recruiting the top stars of the sport for tournaments, exhibitions, and promotional events. Pabst, Schlitz, Blatz, and Stroh's, Budweiser, Hamm's, Falstaff, and Ballantine sponsored men's and women's teams alike. The marriage of beer and bowling was cemented in such German-populated cities as St. Louis, Detroit, and Milwaukee.

Bowling flourished during World War II thanks to defense employment and travel limitations imposed by rationing. Bowling centers were within easy reach by car, bus, train, or subway. Defense workers with pockets jingling turned to bowling as a recreational outlet and a release from the emotional strains of the times. Women bowled more as a result of the stress engendered in their new role as "Rosie the Riveter." Because factories operated around the clock, leagues started at all hours to accommodate the various shifts. Movie actors and star bowlers visited service bases to instruct or exhibit their skills. Bowling became one of the most popular entertainments for

▲ TOP: Outdoor bowling was popular, as this Hollywood publicity photo from 1928 shows. ABOVE: Women bowlers bought war bonds to pay for bombers such as Miss Nightingale II, shown being christened at Clover Field, Santa Monica, Calif., in 1945.

▶ Army aircraft insignia patch from the 19th Bombardment Squadron.

servicemen. Responding out of strong patriotism, bowlers bought war bonds in huge amounts. Bowling centers were the sites of fund-raising projects for the Red Cross, USO, and other aid groups. Female bowlers were galvanized by the Women's International Bowling Congress's "Buy a Bomber" and "Wings of Mercy" programs, which resulted in the purchase of "Miss WIBC" and "Miss Nightingale" (I, II, and III), Douglas A-20 attack bombers, as well as various pieces of equipment and ambulances. In 1942, the Bowlers Victory Legion was formed to provide recreational equipment for the armed forces and rehabilitation funds for patients in veterans hospitals.

What was to come next in the aftermath of the war would revolutionize bowling: the automatic pinsetter. Pinboys had been the backbone of the industry, the

▲ The pinboy and the machine that replaced him. TOP: The dexterity of palming all ten pins at once earned top pay for efficient pinboys. ABOVE: The 1946 AMF Automatic Pinspotter that revolutionized the bowling industry.

◄ LEFT: "Pin"-up girl, Los Angeles, 1930. Note vintage wooden balls and pins.

► OPPOSITE: As evidenced in this 1946 photo, the game had mellowed, and women were attracted by softer lighting, soundproofing, and more space for bowlers and spectators to relax.

unsung heroes. An indispensable part of the game, they were also a problem that inhibited bowling's growth, for they were hard to get, tough to control, and more difficult to keep. Although many successful business and professional men had been pinboys in their first jobs, that function was performed most often by truants and those bordering on the criminal and alcoholic. Any upscale teenager in his right mind would rather find safer employment behind a soda fountain than dodge sixteen-pound mineralite balls and flying pins game after game. Pinboys were in short supply during wartime. Automatic pinsetters exploded the game wide open. The machines did the job better, cheaper, and more dependably than the pinboy. No longer were there human limitations to consider, and this made bowling a 24-hour recreation in some cities. The first machine to meet sanctioned approval was invented by Gottfried Schmidt and developed by the American Machine & Foundry Co. Displayed at a tournament in Buffalo in 1946, it wasn't approved until 1952, when twelve machines were installed at Bowl-O-Drome in Mt. Clemens, Michigan. AMF's nearest competitor, Brunswick, was still three years away from producing a pinsetter. Technology was booming, and America's postwar love affair with suburbia created more space for larger centers and more business. The installation of air conditioning enabled lanes to remain open year-round, including the hot summer months. Bowling alleys provided an ideal hangout for clean-cut teenagers of that era, and their parents enjoyed the social aspects as well, making use of the lounges and restaurants. Some centers even provided nursery care for children while housewives bowled in coffee and doughnut leagues. Family togetherness thrived. Bowling was healthful and fun.

An estimated 12 million people bowled in 1940. That figure doubled by the early '50s. The game was depicted on covers of national magazines, earning its niche in Americana. Coincidentally, television arrived on the scene at about the same time as the innovative pinspotter. Due to a paucity of suitable ideas for television programming in those early days, bowling was called upon to fill the slot. It was one of the few sports easily shot and inexpensively produced. Television brought the people's sport into the home, proving that it was a game for everyone. *Championship Bowling, Bowling Stars, Pin Point,* and *Make That Spare* were a few of the shows seen coast to coast. The ineffable Milton Berle was emcee of *Jackpot Bowling,* which showed professional bowlers trying to roll the most consecutive strikes. The prize money was enormous, and this booty attracted some of the best bowlers. Therm Gibson of Detroit won a whopping $75,000 in 1961 for six consecutive strikes on the show. *Celebrity Bowling* pitted movie, television, and recording stars against each other. Frankly, the between-frames chatter had as much appeal as the bowling. Well-known celebrities doing something millions of ordinary people regularly did kept the show on for years. The zany *Bowling for Dollars* had a down-to-earth appeal, although critics universally panned it. Raw novices won simple prizes such as an oil change, a coupon for pizza, a gallon of ice cream, or a car wash for as little as two strikes in a row. Since those seminal days, the Professional Bowlers' Tour is now a staple on television. The ever-increasing purses attract the cream of today's talented keglers.

Bowling is not only one of the most popular year-round sports in America, it is also one of the most organized. Ten million men, women, and youngsters bowl in leagues every week, with three million more open bowlers. Incredibly, there are another 60 million casual bowlers who frequent local lanes several times a year. The latest fad to increase bowling attendance is known as "Rock & Bowl," where rock and roll music is turned up, the lights are turned down, and young urbanites can bowl till the break of dawn. There are no barriers of age, sex, race, physical or mental handicaps in bowling. It crosses all levels of income, education, and religious beliefs and serves as a true melting pot of recreational life—not only in the United States but also worldwide. That's something to shake a kegel at!

▶ RIGHT: Fifties styling attracted new clientele in Brunswick's modern lanes.

Bowling centers drew raves for their architectural splendor in the late '30s and '40s. Similarities to movie palaces were no coincidence, as evidenced by S. Charles Lee's work on the Tower Bowl. Neon lights and exterior signage beckoned from the street, day or night. The postwar exodus to suburbia eliminated the confines of city space as architects unleashed imaginative designs on the open landscape. California— where land was plentiful and cheap, the business climate receptive, and where sprawling freeways were arteries to the suburbs—became the role model for the country. The leading exponent of bowling alley architecture was the firm of Powers, Daly and De- Rosa. Their designs featured flamboyant exteriors, cavernous concourses, lavish lounges, and ostentatious entryways incorporating all the latest materials and organic shapes of the '50s. Buildings were transformed from the cold and cumbersome to the sleek and inviting, spawning surrounding coffee shops, supermarkets, and car washes. Prosperity showed up as architectural space and modern signage. This was what utopia looked like—architecture designed for and used by the masses. Modernism directed suburbanites to enter and bowl a few frames.

▲ Circular shapes were a popular motif in bowling signage. Downey Bowl, California. (Photo: Tim Street-Porter, 1978)

▶ OPPOSITE: Tower Bowl, San Diego, California. Designed by S. Charles Lee in the streamlined modern style of the early 1930s. (Photo: © John Margolies/ESTO, 1979)

▲ Forties signage of Wagon Wheel Bowl,
Oxnard, California.

► Ordered design
of Panorama Bowl,
Van Nuys, California.

▲ Classic shapes
of Paradise Lanes,
New Orleans, Louisiana.

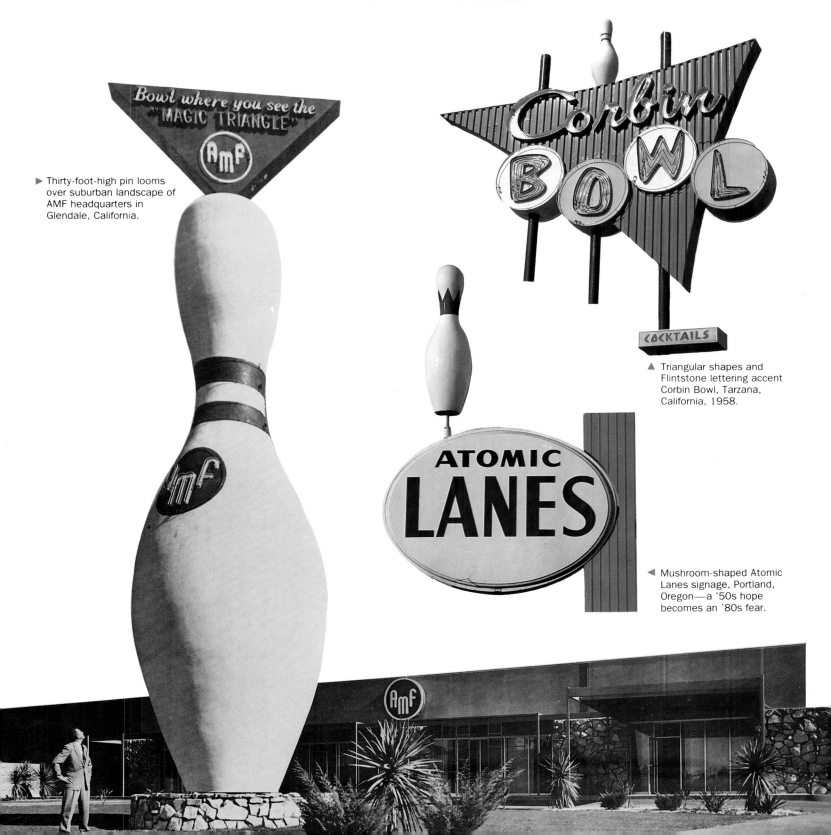

▶ Thirty-foot-high pin looms over suburban landscape of AMF headquarters in Glendale, California.

▲ Triangular shapes and Flintstone lettering accent Corbin Bowl, Tarzana, California, 1958.

◀ Mushroom-shaped Atomic Lanes signage, Portland, Oregon—a '50s hope becomes an '80s fear.

Bowl where you see the "MAGIC TRIANGLE"

AMF

Corbin BOWL

COCKTAILS

ATOMIC LANES

▲ Lonely art deco of Mt. Holly Bowling Center, New Jersey.

▲ Bird Bowl featuring 40 automatic pinspotted lanes, Kansas City, Missouri

▲ Kinetic signage of Sheridan Recreation, Mineola, New York.

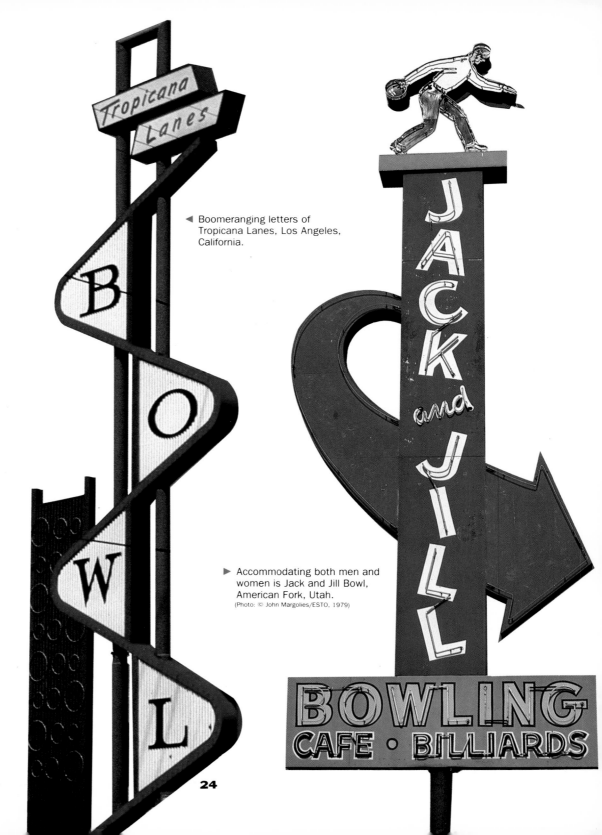

◄ Boomeranging letters of Tropicana Lanes, Los Angeles, California.

► Accommodating both men and women is Jack and Jill Bowl, American Fork, Utah.
(Photo: © John Margolies/ESTO, 1979)

24

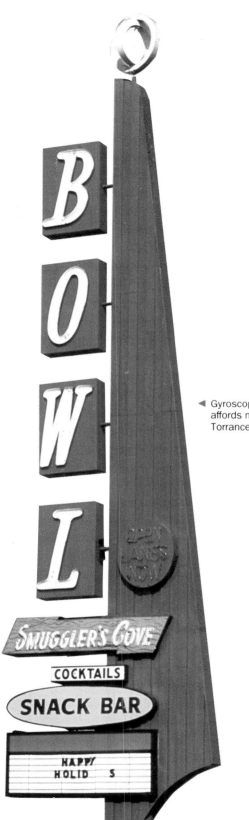

▲ Playful Bowlarama beckons in New Orleans, Louisiana.

◄ Gyroscopic-topped bowling standard affords much information, Torrance, California.

◄ Mission Bowl with speared pin and skewered shapes, Oceanside, California.

▼ Vogue Recreation in Detroit, Michigan, blends soft curves and bowling ball forms with its '30s art deco facade.

▶ OPPOSITE: Opening night at the fashionable Llo-Da-Mar, Santa Monica, California; so named for its owners— actor Harold Lloyd, pro bowlers Ned Day and Hank Marino.

▲ A fond portrait of famed Hollywood Legion Lanes, California, before its demise in 1985.

▲ Ball falls from gravitational pull at Ala Moana Bowl, Lihue, Kauai.

▲ Argyle-inspired signage of suburban Cove Bowl, Norwich, Vermont.

MATCHBOOKS
POST CARDS & PINUPS

As small space ads, matchbooks did the job of a much larger promotion. The publicity generated by matchbooks was subtle and light-handed, definitely not hard sell. But the effect was far-reaching in a subliminal sense for these hidden persuaders. Everytime a match was used, the image on the cover was reinforced. It was a cost-effective use of advertising money for any business, including the bowling establishment. Millions of matches and covers were produced to serve this need before the advent of reusable and later disposable lighters. That many matches accounts for a lot of smokers, and for the tensions of bowling smoking was a pacifier. As with anything else that was given for free, they were collected by people from places they had been. This mini-artform survives. In spite of printing quality limitations, matchbooks still stand as striking examples of early graphics in their simplicity and design.

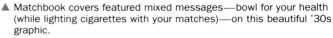

▲ Matchbook covers featured mixed messages—bowl for your health (while lighting cigarettes with your matches)—on this beautiful '30s graphic.

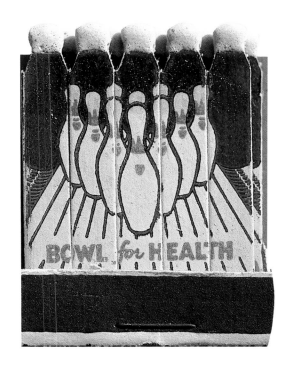

▲ Under the gaze of a close-up lens, the mundane becomes rather "striking" on these matchbook packets, showing interior and exterior views.

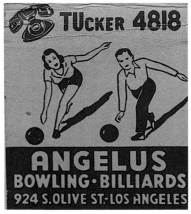

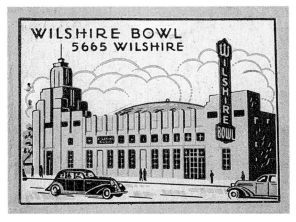

▲ The small space advertisements that matchbooks provided enhanced bowling's appeal beyond the alleys.

▶ OPPOSITE: Thirties architecture was highlighted on these cover blow-ups from Los Angeles area lanes.

Hollywood Recreation
1539 N. VINE ST.
HOLLYWOOD, CALIF.

BOWLING • BILLIARDS • COCKTAIL LOUNGE • CAFE

A Complete Air Change every 4½ Minutes!

WILSHIRE - LA BREA RECREATION

BOWLING

COCKTAILS COFFEE SHOP

737 SO. LA BREA • PHONE YOrk 5296 • 28 BOWLING ALLEYS

Free Paved Parking Lot

COCKTAILS 20TH CENTURY RECREATION COFFEE SHOP

20TH CENTURY RECREATION --
3721 SOUTH WESTERN
PHONE VE-4158

POST CARDS

Why write a long letter when a post card will do? From the turn of the century, the post card offered the most inexpensive means to relay a simple message to a friend. The popular theme of bowling emerged on post cards as concepts for fond hellos, humorous replies, or points of interest across the country. The linen-finish cards lent an air of fine art at sensible prices. Unlike letters, post cards were often found tacked up on walls, magnetized to refrigerators, or filed into shoeboxes with other memorable souvenirs. They were a testament to bowling's charm and popularity throughout the country. The sport put more than a few towns on the map. I would much rather receive a post card in the mail than a bill—anytime!

◄ German commemorative stamp honoring age-old tradition.

▲ Bowling's most obvious puns put to use in this 1957 post card by Tichnor Bros., Boston, Massachusetts.

► OPPOSITE: Vintage bowling post cards from 1912 (top row) to mid-century (bottom) kept friends in touch by mail.

PINUP ART

Sex was used to sell many things over the years—magazines, refrigerators, cars, and even bowling. An attractive female was once a suitable enticement for any business promotion. Women were put on pedestals in every possible situation. Men fantasized over illustrated or photographed women and literally pinned the images up on their walls. Companies that produced calendars knew these facts of life very well. The mind's image of that pristine calendar with its pinup girl hanging in a greasy auto mechanic's garage is one nostalgic thought that comes to mind. The pinups of the '30s and '40s generally had clothes on (skimpy though they were), which stirred viewers' fertile fantasies more about what was hidden than what was exposed. We've come a long way since then in our view and treatment of women, but we should not therefore disregard what once was true. The images were naive, innocent, and idealistic and should be appreciated from that perspective.

▲ *Sally in Our Alley* was painted by Walt Otto for the Osborne Company in the 1940s. This colortype married pinup art and bowling, printed with a variety of colored backgrounds to suit your needs.

▶ OPPOSITE: *Striking*—Greta, a shapely sweater girl from the '40s shown on her way to a perfect game. Painted by D'Ancona for Louis F. Dow Company, St. Paul, Minnesota.

34

STRIKING

GRETA-

D'ANCONA

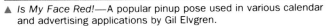

▲ *Is My Face Red!*—A popular pinup pose used in various calendar and advertising applications by Gil Elvgren.

▲ ABOVE RIGHT: *Spare?*—This is but one in a series of highly chauvinistic pinup scenarios featuring a publicly embarrassed woman losing her panties; artist unknown and for good reason.

▶ Stylized graphic matchbook art shown at lower right.

▶ *Pic*—A lusty magazine created to boost morale for the armed forces during wartime, featuring a model whose talents include bowling.

▶ *Laff*—Another tabloid using women and humor to relieve national tension—sex masquerading as bowling.

▼ Uncompromising view of pinup girl hitting the deck on this Pan Pacific Lanes matchbook cover—alley oops!

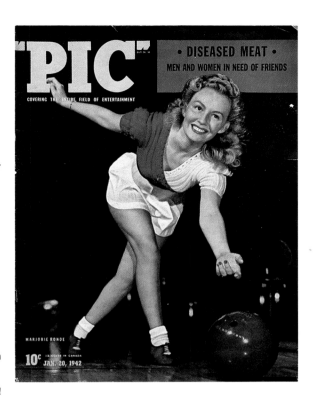

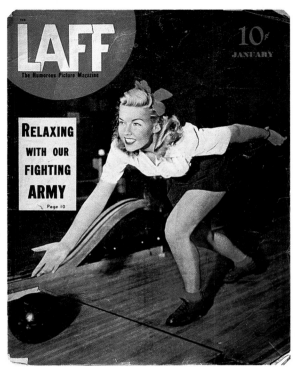

BOWLING SHIRTS
PATCHES & LABELS

Bowling shirts are this sport's proof of the engrossing sense of humor of its patrons. Bowling was organized fun, and each team had its own special identity. No nickname was too strange, no image too ridiculous. These were the workingman's uniform during gametime. The shirts were reasonably priced then, though well-made of fine fabrics—rayon challis, linen, or gabardine. The embroidery work on the shirt backs was truly exceptional. As with so many other garments, polyester double-knits have replaced the natural materials of yesterday. Simple silkscreening of a team name and company logo now suffices. The older shirts have become collectible commodities, especially the more humorous or historical designs with ornate embroidery. Change identities as you change shirts. Why not assume a new character and answer to "Bob" from the Singing Legionaires for the day? Give one to a friend whose personality matches the shirt's message, name, or graphic. Or maybe a shirt that is the antithesis of the recipient's nature would be more fun.

▶ Close-up of pin man embroidery from White City Bowling team, Ogden, Utah.

▲ Classic and humorous designs of commercially sponsored bowling-team shirt backs.

▶ AT RIGHT: The happy couple sport natty Nat Nast's new line of shirts featuring free-swing vented action-backs with two-tone color, 1952.

▲ A sense of humor and innocent simplistic graphics add to the playful competition between teams.

▲ Vintage, collectible bowling-team shirts display colorful embroidery and eye-catching designs.

▶ FOLLOWING SPREAD: Isolated embroidery shows the range of imagery, workmanship, and comic relief.

◄ Sun Lithograph

► Jay Dee's Sporting Goods

▲ Smile with Nile, Seattle

◄ L.A. Toros from Steve Nagy's shirt

▼ The Jokers

▲ Vegas Vic

◄ Valley Cavern

▲ Berry's Funeral Home

▶ Rock and Roll Bowling

◀ Reddy Kilowatt

▲ Diablo Bowling Association

▶ The Carrot Tops,
a team of red-headed
bowlers

▶ Woodmen of the World,
a fraternal organization

▲ From the generic shirt back, specific team-member names or nicknames continued the humorous tradition to the front left pocket, as seen above.

► AT RIGHT: King Louie's embroidered logo is found on the right-hand point of the collar.

▲ Primitive art, inventive lettering, and a good laugh
combine to form the elements of a classic bowling shirt.

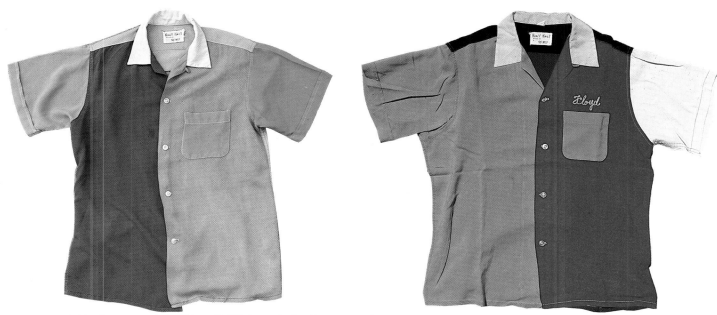

▲ Nat Nast created the ''Krazy Kwilt'' line out of pattern remnants of solid-colored shirts for this wild rainbow effect.

▲ Both the promotional tie and the hand-knitted sweater completed the best-dressed bowler's wardrobe.

Patches and badges rewarding individual or team efforts dressed up bowling shirts like the service decorations of war heroes. They lent an element of achievement and status to the bearer. Arm patches were given for unusual performances and scoring levels reached in sanctioned league and tournament play by the American Bowling Congress, and for both the women's and junior divisions as well. Just like merit badges of the Boy and Girl Scouts, authentic patches boosted confidence and gave strong encouragement of steady progress to youngsters and oldsters alike. Bowling's future expansion was dependent on its youth, so the leagues did not want to risk losing novices to frustration. The quality of the early patches would be difficult and expensive to match today. Gone are the multicolored, intricately designed shapes of old. Today single-colored patches or iron-ons are the norm. Being awarded a gold-threaded 300 game badge made it a proud day for anyone.

► Brightly colored patches, provided as advertisements by local businesses, were given for high scores in tournament play or personal plateau awards and emblazoned team shirts, adding prestige to already well-adorned garments.

▲ OPPOSITE AND ABOVE: American Bowling Congress patches were
◄ awarded to qualified bowlers in league-sanctioned play.

▲ Chief Halftown, a full-blooded Seneca Indian, was a top television
bowling personality in Philadelphia in 1960, originating junior
bowling tournaments and various clinics.

LABELS

Labels provide quite a bit of information if you are looking for that. It is how we shop. Labels offer us status and are required on everything we purchase. They are usually an incidental part of the item bought, but even the commonplace becomes noticeably interesting when blown up many times its normal size. In this fast-paced world we often do not stop to smell the roses nor do we stop to look at labels. This microscopic world displays square inches packed with fluid lettering, well-conceived designs, and memorable logos. I admire the effort and expense that went into these shirt labels. They are the signature of the manufacturer that validates the product. For the collectible in signed artwork, enjoy the who's who of bowling-wear. Are you a S, M, L, or XL?

▲ Vintage bowling shirt labels help identify collectible clothing and inspire high scores.

CELEBRITY BOWLERS

Bowling boomed in California from the turn of the century to well into the '50s, specifically in Southern California—home of movie stars, television celebrities, and magical Hollywood. In the late '30s, Hollywood studio publicity mills churned out stories and photos of their current stars participating in the newest craze—bowling. From Tyrone Power to Harold Lloyd, Alice Faye to Carole Lombard, everyone bowled. Even cameramen, grips, and gofers behind the scenes by day joined celebrity-sponsored studio teams by night. M-G-M wasted no time capitalizing on the sport, producing two Pete Smith shorts entitled *Strikes and Spares* and *Set 'Em Up* that featured Andy Varipapa, the greatest trick bowler the game has known. He was an all-star champion bowler, but tricks such as converting 7–10 splits by using two balls at once or rolling hook balls through the legs of gorgeous pinup girls made him famous. As a way to parlay lucrative sports salaries into retirement nest eggs, athletes invested in prospering bowling centers, a group that included such baseball notables as Ted Williams, Yogi Berra, Nellie Fox, and Sherm Lawler. Even presidents and politicians took time to keep fit. You most certainly are bowling in good company!

▲ This 1946 cover of *Bowler's Journal* features actor Ronald Reagan and his first wife, Jane Wyman, watching pins fly at Sunset Bowl, Los Angeles; looking on are Rosemary Lane and Tom MacAvity.

▶ OPPOSITE: Another contract actor for 20th Century-Fox, Tyrone Power, shows good form on this sports cover.

Bowler

AND SPORTS REVIEW

15¢

BOWLING

Articles By

Ben Decker

Bob McGraw

Edna Cobb

"Bugs" Woodard

George Nelson

Frank Ferguson

•

News from the Bowling Alleys

●

April, 1938

Vol. 1   Number 3

Tyrone Power, 20th Century-Fox actor, keeps in physical trim by improving his average which is already quite good.

▲ Sam Snead tees off for Dick Weber and Jan McNeil.

▲ Lefty Governor Earl Warren opens Tournament.

▲ ABOVE: Xavier Cugat promotes a Red Cross blood drive with Uncle Sam in New York City, 1943.

▶ BOTTOM RIGHT: Joe E. Brown discusses fine points of bowling—which has the larger diameter, his ball or his mouth?

◀ BELOW: Fred contemplates escape as Wilma bursts bubble in favor of clean dishes. (© Hanna-Barbera)

56

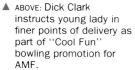 ABOVE: Dick Clark instructs young lady in finer points of delivery as part of "Cool Fun" bowling promotion for AMF.

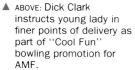 ABOVE RIGHT: Dick Van Dyke introduces ball to pin in scene from *Divorce American Style.*

▶ RIGHT: Don Adams as Maxwell Smart strikes pose for publicity.

▶ FAR RIGHT: Art Linkletter and Girl Scout urge teenagers to participate in a national bowling event to "Bowl Down Cancer."

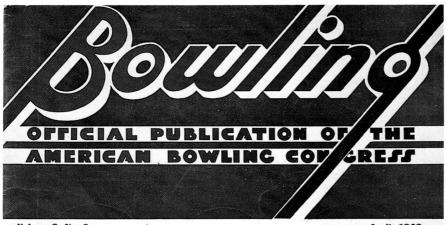

▲ Bob Hope holds slight advantage over Jerry Colonna in this mug shot from 1943.

► RIGHT TOP & BOTTOM: Presidential keglers keep in shape. Southpaw Harry Truman had lanes installed in the White House; Richard Nixon takes advantage of them.

NEW PHILLIES

JACKPOT BOWLING

Starring MILTON BERLE

featuring the WORLD'S GREATEST BOWLERS

MILTON BERLE M.C.'s two big matches every week for strikes only . . . 1st match—$5,000.00 Jackpot for six consecutive strikes . . . winner rolls against **"KING OF THE HILL"** in feature match for Jackpot beginning at $25,000.00. Each week $5,000.00 is added to Jackpot of feature match if it isn't hit! This means from time to time the Jackpot will be over

$100,000.00

STARTS SEPT. 19th EVERY MONDAY NITE NBC TELEVISION

PHILLIES LEADS ALL CIGAR BRANDS IN SALES! BE SURE YOU HAVE A FULL LINE OF PHILLIES

▲ NBC's promotional poster for television's new *Jackpot Bowling* has Milton Berle (a.k.a. Milton Bowl) protecting pins, 1960.

▶ Jane Withers, Mickey Rooney, and pro bowler Hank Marino line up their sights at Llo-Da-Mar Lanes, 1941.

BOWLING GRAPHICS

The visual possibilities of bowling's arresting images were endless. This wholesome sport was enjoyed by entire families, including all races and religions. Communicators, desirous of reaching the broadest possible cross section of the American population, hit upon bowling as a vehicle to carry their messages. Advertising campaigns married beer and bowling, cigarettes and bowling, even candy and soft drinks and bowling for the younger generation of consumers. Record albums and sheet music used puns in word and illustration. The forms and shapes of the ball and pin world lent themselves easily to the two-dimensional graphic arts. It was a brand-new theme to milk, a new wave of design to ride, and certainly a marketable image to sell. Publicity photos of incredible stunts surfaced in newspapers for human-interest stories. Magazine covers and movie posters brought bowling awareness indirectly to the public eye via the newsstands and movie theaters. Proof of bowling's tremendous popularity lies in these varied (pin) points of purchase.

▲ Photographer Ralph Bartholomew was chosen for the 1948 Kodak ad campaign directed toward the burgeoning adolescent market. His images depicted teenagers of the postwar era engaged in all-American activities. (© Ralph Bartholomew, courtesy of Daniel Wolf Gallery, New York)

▶ OPPOSITE: The U.S. War Production Board pumped efficiency through patriotism in this 1942 poster satirizing Hitler, Mussolini, and Tojo. At bowling centers proprietors literally had these enemy faces painted on pins so one could ''slap Tojo'' or ''strike Hitler.''

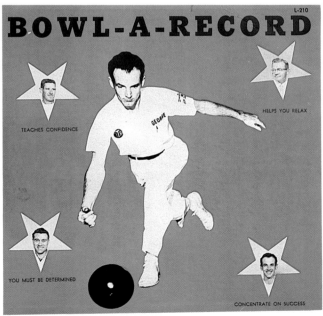

▲ Long-playing records utilized bowling graphics to sell product. ABOVE LEFT: Mary Kay Place, playing Loretta Haggers of Mary Hartman fame, poses outside Picwood Bowl in West Los Angeles. ABOVE RIGHT: The J. Geils Band issued their ''greatest hits'' via posed photo of strike in progress. LEFT: Bowl-A-Record provided self-help by using guided imagery techniques.

▶ OPPOSITE: Sheet music from the '30s and '40s extolling the virtues of the new craze of bowling.

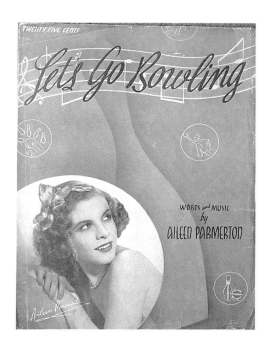

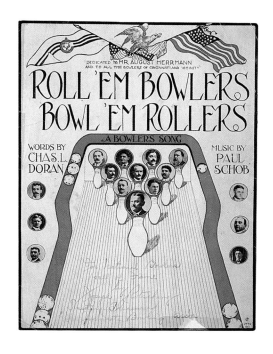

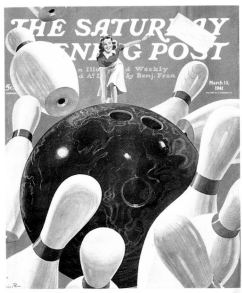

BEGINNING A
NEW SERIAL **BLOOD ON THE MOON**

▲ Magazine covers of the '40s decade display the graphics, humor, and inherent frustration of the sport.

▶ OPPOSITE: Trick bowler Andy Varipapa and Ned Day teamed together in the Pete Smith short, *Set 'Em Up*, in 1936.

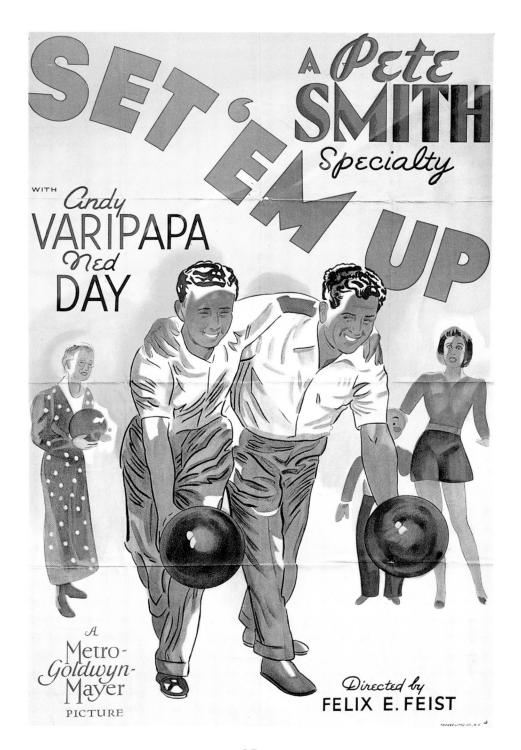

▲ Harry Von Zell and Bill Goodwin mix the pleasures of beer and bowling in this 1950 Pabst Beer ad.

▲ Thematic illustration graces this advertisement for Kentucky Tavern.

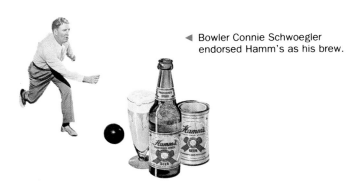

◀ Bowler Connie Schwoegler endorsed Hamm's as his brew.

▶ Winston cigarettes pinned down the bowling market.

GOOD SCORES REQUIRE *Energy*

CURTISS CANDIES ARE RICH IN DELICIOUS *FOOD-ENERGY*

CHAMPIONS in every line find it necessary constantly to replenish used up energy. Much as skill counts in bowling, you can't let your energy lag for an instant. One listless delivery may keep you out of the prize money.

You get real food-energy at all times and for all occasions in delicious, satisfying Curtiss Candies. They are *rich in dextrose—the sugar your body uses directly for energy.* They help sustain your energy when you need it most.

For a real taste thrill and a food-energy boost, treat yourself right now to a delicious easy-to-eat Curtiss Candy Bar. Only 5¢.

. . . Illustrated here is one of the earliest forms of bowling (about the year 1200 A.D.). The object is to lay the ball as close to the cones as possible.

. . . Bowling has gone a long ways in the intervening years as is evidenced by the up-to-date, attractive alleys illustrated here.

CURTISS CANDY Baby Ruth 5¢
CURTISS CANDY Butterfinger 5¢
CURTISS CANDY JOLLY JACK 5¢

RICH IN DEXTROSE THE SUGAR YOUR BODY USES DIRECTLY FOR ENERGY

CURTISS CANDY COMPANY, CHICAGO, ILLINOIS

▲ Curtis Candy Company promoted food energy (and lots of sugar) to bolster bowling scores.

The *All-Family Drink!*

"fresh up" with Seven-Up!

Bright and lively 7-Up is "right down your alley" whether you're out bowling with the family . . . or having your fun at home. Crystal-clear and sparkling, 7-Up is so pure, so good, so wholesome that folks of all ages can "fresh up" often!

Buy 7-Up by the CASE!
—or in the handy 7-Up Family Pack of 24 bottles. Family supply, easy-lift center handle, easy-to-store.

You like it . . . it likes you!

▲ The idyllic all-American family drank 7up to quench that bowling thirst.

▲ One of Andy Varipapa's most famous trick shots: a right hook through a row of nine pinup girls to knock the 7 pin.

◄ *Bowling Magazine*'s cover illustrations showed typical predicaments of the weekly bowlers.

▼ BELOW: Coca-Cola lifted sagging spirits and refreshed sports enthusiasts.

RIGHT: Two unorthodox bowling promotions. TOP: Frances du Bay guides horse, Melody Lady, to foul line, 1952.
(Photo courtesy *San Francisco Examiner*)

BELOW: Mike Skrovan (in Hawaiian shirt) built this wacky car in 1949 to promote his bowling center in Cleveland.

TROPHIES
AWARDS & JEWELRY

Trophies and awards are given as records of victory and achievement for athletic feats. The bowling industry used that custom as a psychological incentive to help players reach their personal plateaus. Awards got bigger and more extravagant as prowess and the game itself grew. The pins, medals, and even diamond-encrusted belt buckles were worn proudly by men while bowling. Women used decorative jewelry to dress up their bowling attire. The awards took on a quiet beauty with their sculptural qualities. Figures were well designed and not just stamped out in generic molds. Medals were ornately crafted and embellished with high-quality materials, which made the owner of such prizes want to wear and display them. The examples illustrated here fall into the category of things they don't make as well as they used to.

▲ Examples of trophies and awards of an era gone by—when
▶ trophies were made well and had great value. The awards display at right is from the American Bowling Congress in Milwaukee.

▲ Intricate designs of belt buckles and medals were at one time imbedded with small-carat diamonds.

▲ Skilled artisans using quality materials produced a wide and colorful variety of awards for bowlers.

GRAVOIS CLASSIC
1932
4 GAMES 854
WON BY
M. SCHULTE

"LUXOR"
MIX FIVE
1946
SOMODY

200
TROJAN BOWL

▲ Brass-plated and sterling silver trophies were
just rewards for winning efforts.

74

▲ Cloisonné pins and enameled buttons are still favorites today among collectors.

◄ OPPOSITE: A beautiful example of an anatomically serene sculpture of a male bowler in mid-release.

▲ Women bowlers wore costume jewelry during the '40s and '50s, including rhodium-finished brooches and Bakelite pins and earrings.

Over the decades, the pleasing forms and beautiful shapes of the sport of bowling have attracted artists and designers throughout the world. The pure organic elements and satisfying proportions of ball to pin have turned up in sculpture, painting, and even in functional furniture. The sheer mathematics of size and spatial relationships in bowling create inherent templates for imagined masterpieces. Bowling awareness has infiltrated our lives. Artists have always absorbed the materials of popular culture, called them to our attention, and reflected them back through means of their artform. Art displays form, beauty, and unusual perceptions of man's creativity in giving birth to something new. The following pieces emanate those very qualities through the widespread influence of bowling——art for bowling's sake.

▶ *Winged Victory* by Anthony Machado, 1981, for Fat City, a San Diego restaurant. His bowling motif is also pervasive in the Los Angeles restaurant Palette, featuring bowling ball vases, columns, and terrazzo floors.

▲ *Blue Bowling Ball* by Edward Ruscha, 1972. Comically religious.
(Oil on canvas, 20 × 24''; collection 1st City National Bank of Houston, Texas.)

▲ *Times Tower Competition* by William Sloan, 1984, made an alley of Times Square. (Courtesy Municipal Arts Society, co-sponsored by the National Endowment for the Arts.)

▲ "Bowling Alley Coffee Table" by Steven Galerkin from 1984 Unofficial Sports Furniture Show. "Erection Set with Balls" by Larry Whiteley, 1985, from "Son of L.A. Apocalypse." (Photos by Ingo Harney, courtesy Whiteley Gallery, L.A.)

▶ Art deco bowler— a square head with a round ball.

▲ *Bowling II* by James Chatelain, 1978. The aggressive vision of an angry bowler.

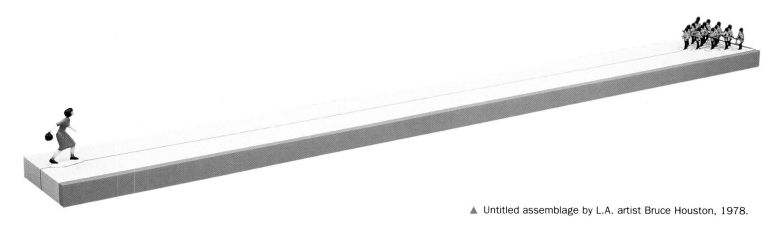

▲ Untitled assemblage by L.A. artist Bruce Houston, 1978.

▲ *Kegelspieler* by German Expressionist painter Niklaus Stoecklin, 1918.

▲ 1955 mosaic on side of bowling alley near L.A. airport.

▲ Pastel drawing of professional bowler in classic form.

▲ *Hercules and Atlas Bowling on the Milky Way* by Thurston Lindberg, 1939. This mural now graces the Detroit lanes used for the ABC Tournament of 1940.

▲ ABOVE: Untitled photo by artist/photographer Jayme Odgers.

▲ "Bowling Ball Bob Uses His Head," 1985 by artist Bob Zoell—cerebral bowling with a frenzy.

▶ AT RIGHT: Illustration from early ad for AMF automatic pinsetters.

Bowlers are as avid as any sports fans come. Judging from the strange and diverse objects produced during bowling's heyday, some bowlers' tastes bordered on the bizarre. Bowling even infiltrated the enthusiasts' everyday lives, as evidenced by functional household items such as lamps, clocks, salt and pepper shakers, and even small planters that exhibit a bowling motif. That these objects became such a pervasive element of their lifestyles indicates that bowlers enjoyed surrounding themselves with their sport's symbology even when not bowling. If laughter is our best medicine, then bowlers should live to a ripe old age. Their complete immersion in and dedication to the sport and their ability to laugh at themselves allayed any frustration that the game produced. These pieces of junque and found art show just that. The commonplace becomes hilarious and the mundane becomes extraordinary when taken out of context and viewed on the printed page. These priceless treasures can be had for a song if you know where to look.

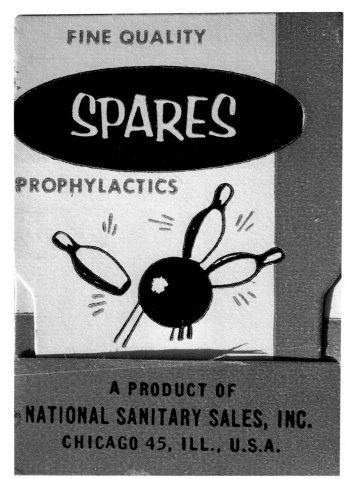

▲ (Fine quality) prophylactics from the '50s. Spare me!

▶ OPPOSITE: ''Railroad Rosie'' and ''Bozo the Bowler''—the definitive booby prizes of trophies, so named for difficult splits and bad scores, 1953.

▲ Suggestive artifacts of a functional nature—naive bowling art at its finest.

▲ A home version of bowling created by Wilson Sporting Goods Company,
using bowling forms to score strikes, spares, and splits, 1942.

▲ Sixties pinball machine glass facade by Bally.

◄ Weathervane from late '50s points out direction to nearest bowling alley.

▲ A rubber squeeze toy from the '40s indoctrinated the young at an early age.

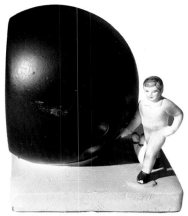

▲ Surreal bookend with oversized ball.

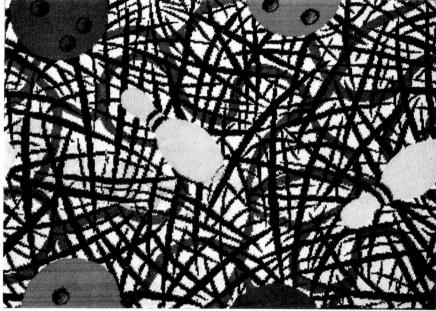

▲ Carpet sample for bowling centers from National Theatre Supply Co., 1960.

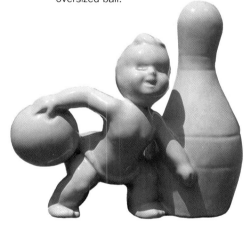

▲ Various planters to arouse bowling interest around the home.

▲ Liquor decanter of comical nature.

◀ Coca-Cola sports clock given as promotional item to clients.

▶ Jim Beam 10-pin bottle, 1958. Plastic versions were made later.

▲ Decorative wallpaper from England shows teens engaged in healthy bowling, 1959.

▶ Portable bowling bar with pump decanter and liqueur glasses, 1940s. Also made in Bakelite plastic.

▲ Bowling bags used to house ball, shoes, and sundries. LEFT: Sylvia Wene was the only woman to bowl three 300 games in sanctioned competition, 1960. RIGHT: Fifties organic doodle pattern debossed in vinyl.

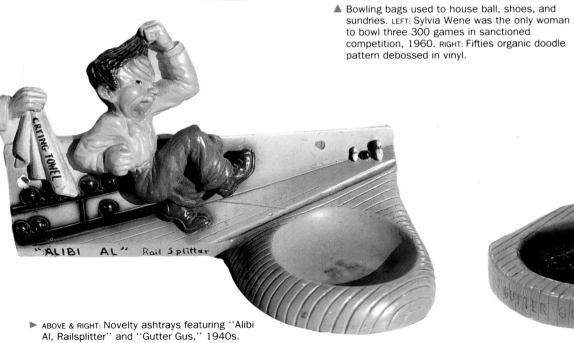

► ABOVE & RIGHT: Novelty ashtrays featuring ''Alibi Al, Railsplitter'' and ''Gutter Gus,'' 1940s.

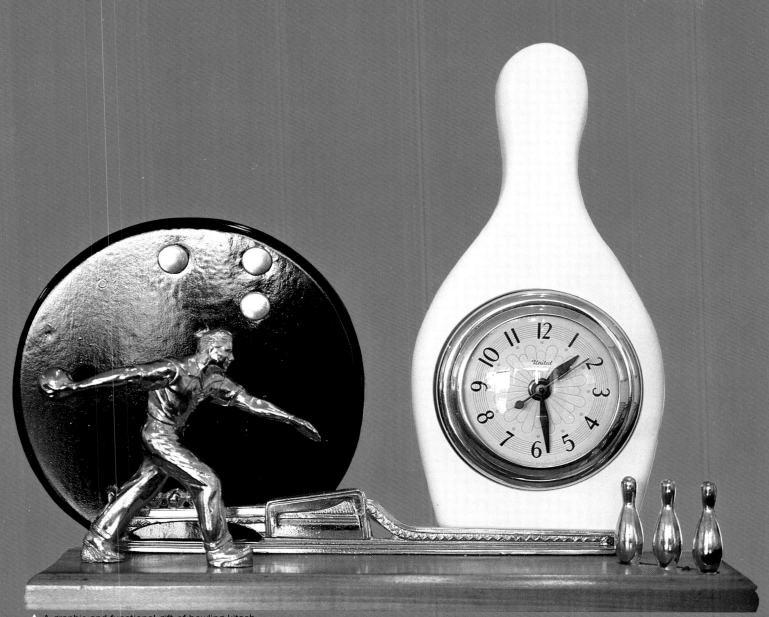

▲ A graphic and functional gift of bowling kitsch.

GLOSSARY OF TERMS

"My mother-in-law was the only one left when I rolled a powder puff down a graveyard." Confusing? It shouldn't be if you've ever caught on to the jargon of bowling. Like every other sport, bowling speaks a colorful language all its own, designed to quicken communications between the millions who enjoy the nation's number one participant sport. Many of the following words will not be new to you, but chances are that you have used them to mean entirely different things.

ANCHOR – last man in a team line-up

APPLE – a bowling ball

BARMAID – a pin hidden behind another; a.k.a. a sleeper

BEDPOSTS – the exasperating 7–10 split; a.k.a. telephone poles, snake eyes, mule ears, or goal posts

BENCHWORK – conversation intended to upset opponents

BODY ENGLISH – anatomical gyrations for wishful steering of the ball after release

BROOKLYN – a ball striking the 1–2 pocket for right-handers, the 1–3 pocket for lefties; a.k.a. crossovers or from the Jersey side

CHEESECAKES – lanes on which it is unusually easy to score

CHERRY – chopping of only front pins in attempt for a spare

CHRISTMAS TREE – 3–7–10 or 2–7–10 splits

CINCINNATI – the 8–10 split

CREEPER – a slow ball; a.k.a. a powder puff

CROW HOPPER – loose, clawlike hand grip on ball

DEAD APPLE – ball having no stuff on it at pin contact; a.k.a. sour apple

DODO – illegally weighted ball producing unusual hook

DUTCHMAN – alternate strikes and spares to yield a score of 200

FOUNDATION – strike in the 9th frame

FRAME – one-tenth of a game; also, box on score sheet in which score is recorded

GOLDEN GATE – 4–6–7–10 split

GRASSHOPPER – good working ball that splashes the pins

GRANDMA'S TEETH – random array of pins left standing

GRAVEYARDS – low-scoring lanes

GUTTERBALL – neither a strike nor a spare; off the side of the lane

HONEY – a good ball

JACK MANDERS – rolling a ball down the middle of a 7–10 split

KEGLER – bowler; from the German sport of kegels

LILY – the near impossible 5–7–10 split

LOFTING – throwing a ball out on the lane beyond the foul line—not popular with bowling proprietors

MAPLES – bowling pins, usually made of maple wood

MOTHER-IN-LAW – the 7 pin, the one hidden in the corner

MURPHY – a baby split, 2–7 or 3–10 pins

PICKET FENCE – 1–2–4–7 or 1–3–6–10 leaves; a.k.a. Chinaman

POISON IVY – the 3–6–10 spare leaves

POODLE – to roll a ball into the gutter

POWDER PUFF – a slow ball

PUMPKIN – a dead ball with no action

RAILROAD – two or more pins left standing with no pins inbetween; a.k.a. grandma's teeth

SCHLEIFER – a thin hit strike where pins seem to fall one by one

SPARE – to clear all remaining pins on second ball of a frame

STRIKE – to clear all pins with first ball of a frame

THROW ROCKS – to roll strike balls

TURKEY – three strikes in a row

WOOLWORTH – a 5–10 split; a.k.a. a dime store

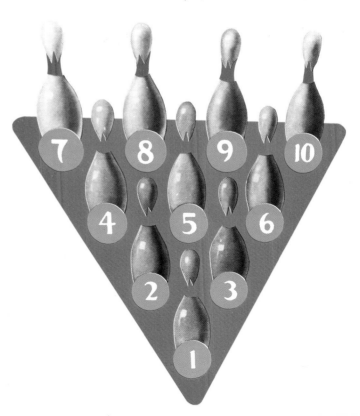

To Jeff Spielberg, whose collection of shirts and gracious loan of time and support helped bring this book into being; Jim Heimann for his moral support and beautiful collection of matchbooks and post cards; Tim Street-Porter and Annie Kelly for photos and post cards; Robert Rodriguez, John Margolies, and Jayme Odgers for use of their photos; Brad Benedict for his wacky objects; Dennis Keeley for his photographic eye; Heather Cummings for design assistance; Ron Larson for his patience and production help; Walton Rawls, my editor at Abbeville, for laying down the lanes for this one; Sarah Jane Freymann; Jerry and Suzie Brownstein; Bill and Jean Gold; Brenda Cain; Off The Wall, L.A.; Skank World, L.A.; Art Deco, L.A.; Metro, San Diego; Loose Threads, Bath, England; Larry Whiteley; S. Charles Lee; Anthony Machado; Edward Ruscha; Bruce Houston; Dennis and Al-lene Rose; Clive Piercy; Stan and Martha Evenson; Jeff and Cathy Lancaster; Rochelle Reed; Alan Hess; Brooke Amber; Roger Handy; Connie Perante for her jewelry; Lee Bond-Upson for Atomic Bowl; Louie Escovar; Tom Kampas; Memories, L.A.; Galaxy 500, L.A.; Elyse Stern; Thomas R. Young and Frank Gargani; Ken Lohman of *Bowling News;* Suzanne Locke of the *San Francisco Examiner;* Laura Broaddus of *New York* magazine; Virginia Dajani; Debbie Davison of the National Bowling Council; Dr. Toohey of L.A. City Library; UCLA Research Library; my extended family ; and Fiona and Pooh.

VERY SPECIAL THANKS

To Bruce Pluckhahn, Ed Marcou, and the staff of the Bowling Hall of Fame and Museum in St. Louis, Missouri, whose Midwestern hospitality, gracious use of their files and archives, and their love of the sport of bowling truly made this book the best it could be.

▲ *"Pinhead Magritte."* (© 1985 SteeleWorks Design, Inc.)